If you're not into trees or slightly silly jokes, I wood leaf now.

The Gentle Genius of Trees

PHILIP BUNTING

CROWN BOOKS
for Young Readers
New York

We hairy humans have a pretty special relationship with trees.

From the very beginning of our tiny kind, we have lived in, around, and with trees. Today, they continue to give us more than you can shake a stick at.

Trees give us:

Shelter.

Food.

Toys.

Fun!

A place to sit.

Books.

Hugs.

Campfires.

Medicine.

Shade.

Trees even give us the air we breathe!
Plant life provides the perfect partner to your
respiratory system* to help keep you puffing along.

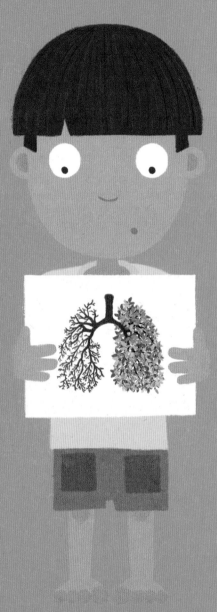

*That's your lungs,
and the various other
parts and pieces that
very kindly help
you breathe.

Every time you take a breath, you inhale oxygen and exhale
carbon dioxide. In turn, trees inhale carbon dioxide and
exhale fresh oxygen for you to breathe in again.

You, me, the birds, the bees, the trees, and the seas—
we're all a part of one beautifully balanced being—
a delicate system of life that exists on and with the earth.

While we eat food to grow, trees fuel up in a slightly different way.
Through a remarkable process called photosynthesis, our foliaged friends
take in most of the nutrients they need to grow by eating thin air!

A tree's leaves very cleverly convert sunlight and air into energy, creating a deliciously sweet sugar called glucose. The tree uses the glucose to grow, heal, and thrive.

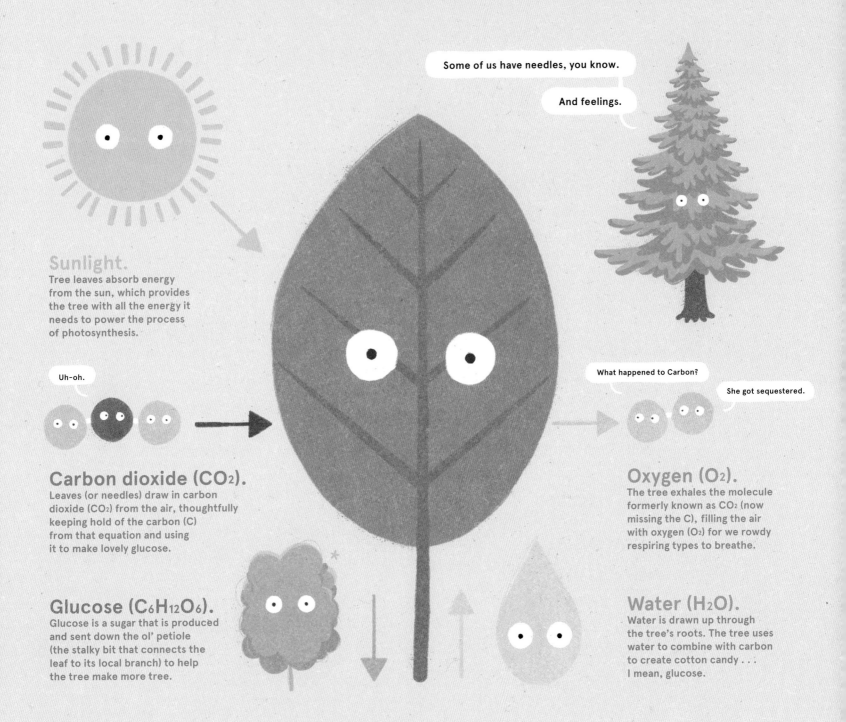

Sunlight.
Tree leaves absorb energy from the sun, which provides the tree with all the energy it needs to power the process of photosynthesis.

Carbon dioxide (CO_2).
Leaves (or needles) draw in carbon dioxide (CO_2) from the air, thoughtfully keeping hold of the carbon (C) from that equation and using it to make lovely glucose.

Glucose ($C_6H_{12}O_6$).
Glucose is a sugar that is produced and sent down the ol' petiole (the stalky bit that connects the leaf to its local branch) to help the tree make more tree.

Oxygen (O_2).
The tree exhales the molecule formerly known as CO_2 (now missing the C), filling the air with oxygen (O_2) for we rowdy respiring types to breathe.

Water (H_2O).
Water is drawn up through the tree's roots. The tree uses water to combine with carbon to create cotton candy . . . I mean, glucose.

* Very serious disclaimer: Artist's** impression only. Glucose does not really look like cotton candy.
** We use the word *artist* in the loosest possible sense. But you get the idea.

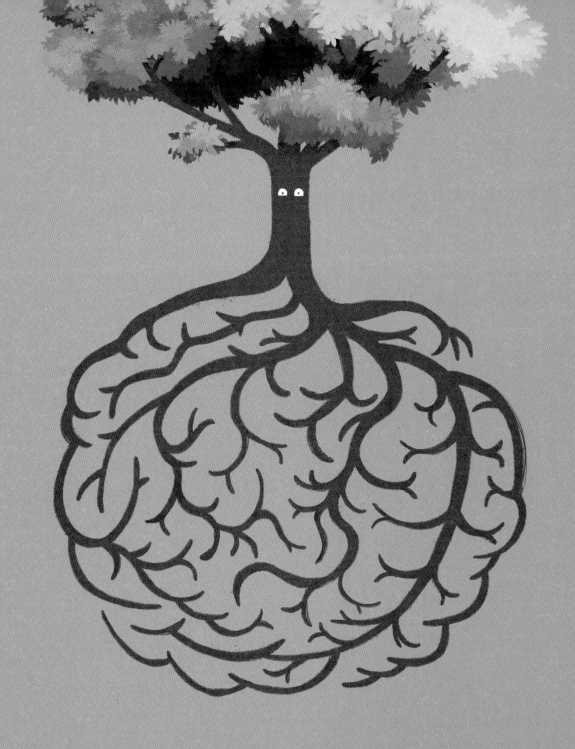

Meanwhile, belowground . . . a tree's roots can grow about four times larger than its crown (its branches and leaves). But these subsoil branches are much more than just supersized drinking straws. You can think of a tree's root system as its brain (only upside down).

This subterranean cerebrum helps trees to do all sorts of wonderful things. You see, trees are very social beings, and they love to be connected to one another.

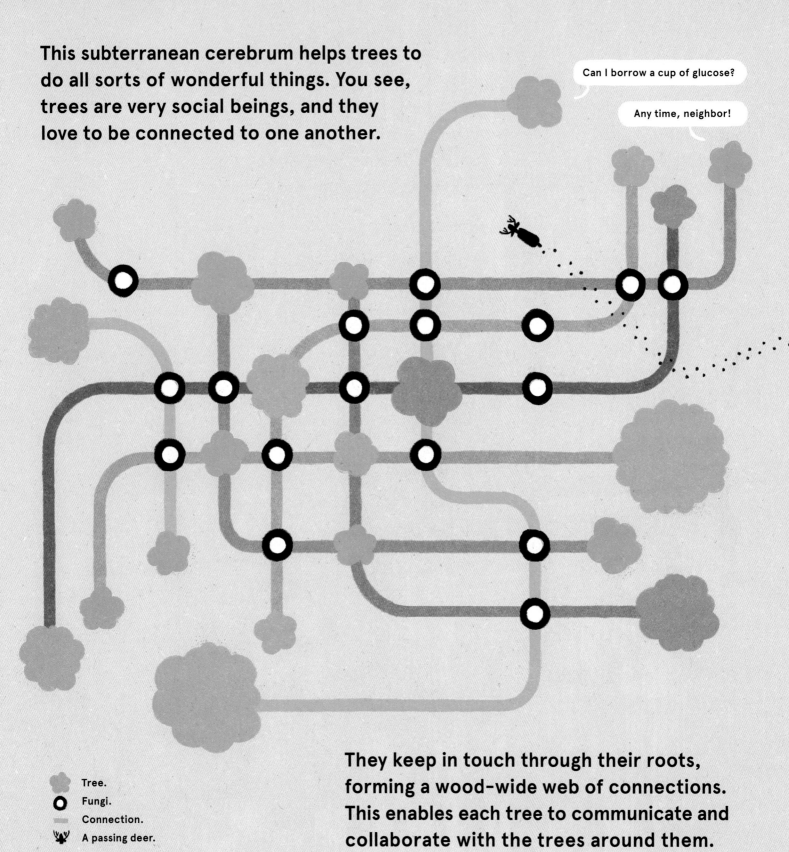

They keep in touch through their roots, forming a wood-wide web of connections. This enables each tree to communicate and collaborate with the trees around them.

For example, if a fellow tree is injured, those around it will send extra nutrients via the wood-wide web to help the unfortunate tree heal itself sooner. Each tree in a forest will do its part for the community. In turn, a connected collective of trees can control their own microclimate, shelter one another from strong winds, and lend each other support through their roots.

They know that what is good for the forest is good for the tree.

Trees also have the ability to warn their barky buddies of impending danger. Let's say a tree suffers a good munching from a local deer. . . .

Munch.

Ouch.

1 Tree munched.
Local deer helps himself to a leafy lunch at the expense of one very unfortunate tree.

2 Warning emitted.
The afflicted tree will send warning signals through the wood-wide web to all the trees in the local network, alerting them to the danger.

3 Other trees react. (Some overreact.)
Once they get the message, the other trees will quickly produce chemicals that make their leaves taste really disgusting.

4 Danger averted.
Soon, all the trees in that neck of the woods will send the foul flavor to their leaves, and the muncher will, well, leave.

To communicate with one another in these ways, trees rely on a very special relationship with some fungal friends. Beneath the soil, fungi and trees create a mutually beneficial bond.

By connecting their mycelium (which are like roots) to the tree's roots, fungi provide trees with the wonderful web of connections to the other trees around them.

In exchange for these connective services, trees feed fungi lovely sweet glucose, which fungi can't make on their own.

But let's get back to the trees.

As a tree grows, its branches search out and grow toward the light. The more light, the more energy (and glucose) the leaves on that branch can produce. So branches growing in more light will receive the most nutrients from the tree and grow the strongest.

In branching out like this, the tree tries many directions and different ways of growing.

If it begins growing a branch toward a darker area (perhaps in the shade of another branch, or into a cave, or in the shadow of a hibernating yeti), the tree will not lose heart.

Rather, it will slow the growth of that branch by pushing its energy and nutrients into the branches that are receiving more sunlight.

In turn, the leaves on the sunny side will produce more glucose, which the tree will use to grow.

A tree will slowly continue to search for the light like this, adjusting when necessary, throughout its long and leafy life.

Fig. 1.
A hungry bird looking for her breakfast.

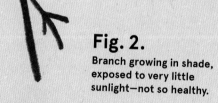

Fig. 2.
Branch growing in shade, exposed to very little sunlight—not so healthy.

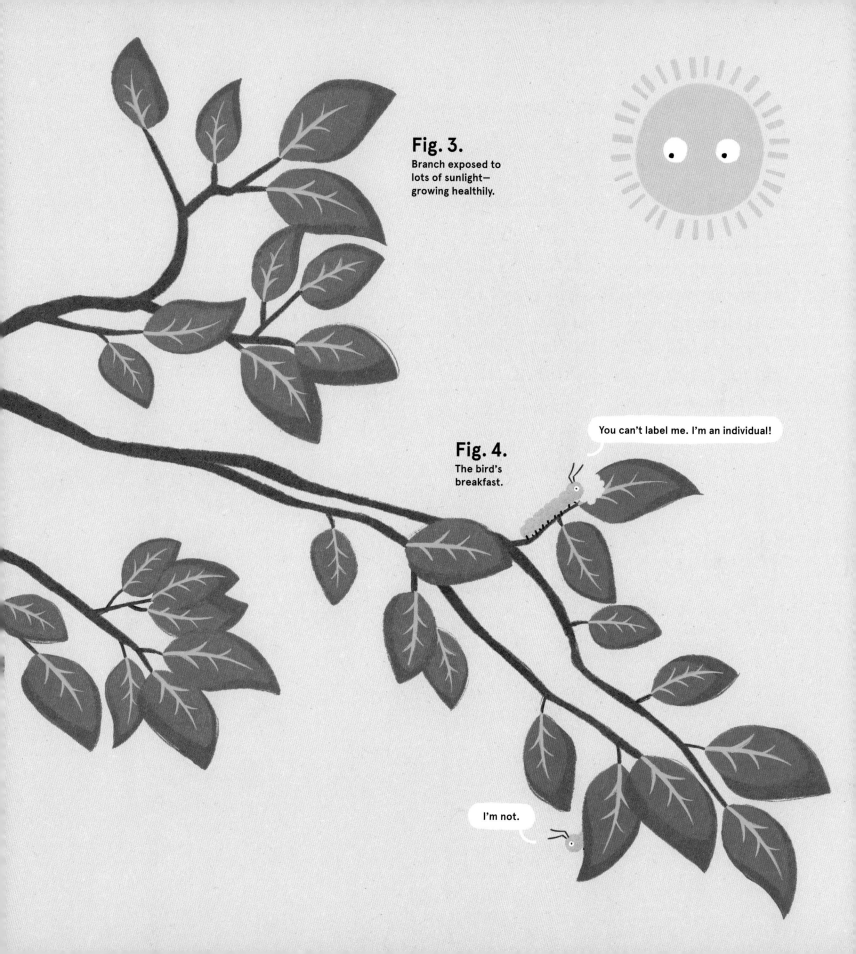

Fig. 3.
Branch exposed to
lots of sunlight—
growing healthily.

Fig. 4.
The bird's
breakfast.

A slower pace of life suits trees very well.

The tree that grows slowly will push its energy into a strong trunk and deeper roots, giving it a lifetime of stability.

The tree that grows too quickly is likely to develop a weak trunk, brittle branches, and shallow roots. Rushed growth means that the cellulose the tree creates to form new wood is spead too thinly, leaving it vulnerable to breaking or falling when tested.

Parent trees assist in slowing the growth of their seedlings by limiting the light the baby trees can receive, helping their young to grow strong, straight trunks. Slowly.

But these mother trees aren't all tough love.
They will feed their seedlings too. As baby trees
often grow beneath the canopy of their parent,
their roots will be connected, allowing the parent to
nurture and send nutrients to their offspring.

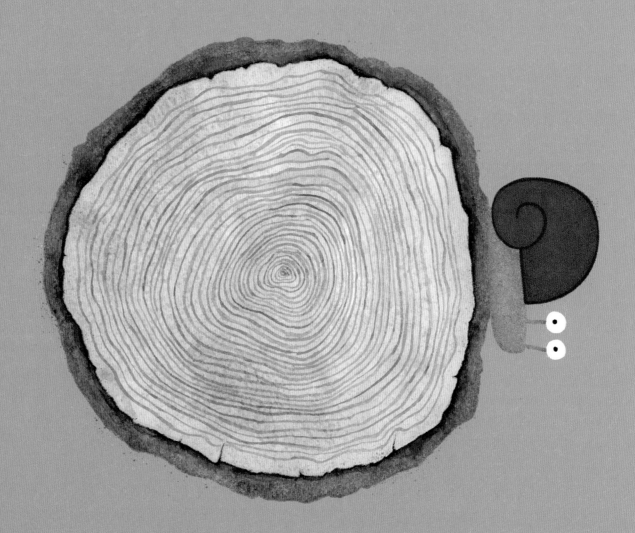

In fact, trees never stop growing. As time ticks slowly by,
they will continue to develop thicker trunks, grow stronger and
longer branches, and regenerate leaves as they need them.
For as long as they are alive, trees seek out the light
and continue to grow.

But to see a healthy old age, trees must be hardy enough to endure whatever the world throws at them. Depending on where they grow, trees must be supple enough to bend in a storm without breaking. . . .

Or tough enough to endure a long
hot drought without giving up.

Or strong enough to carry great loads
of snow without giving in.

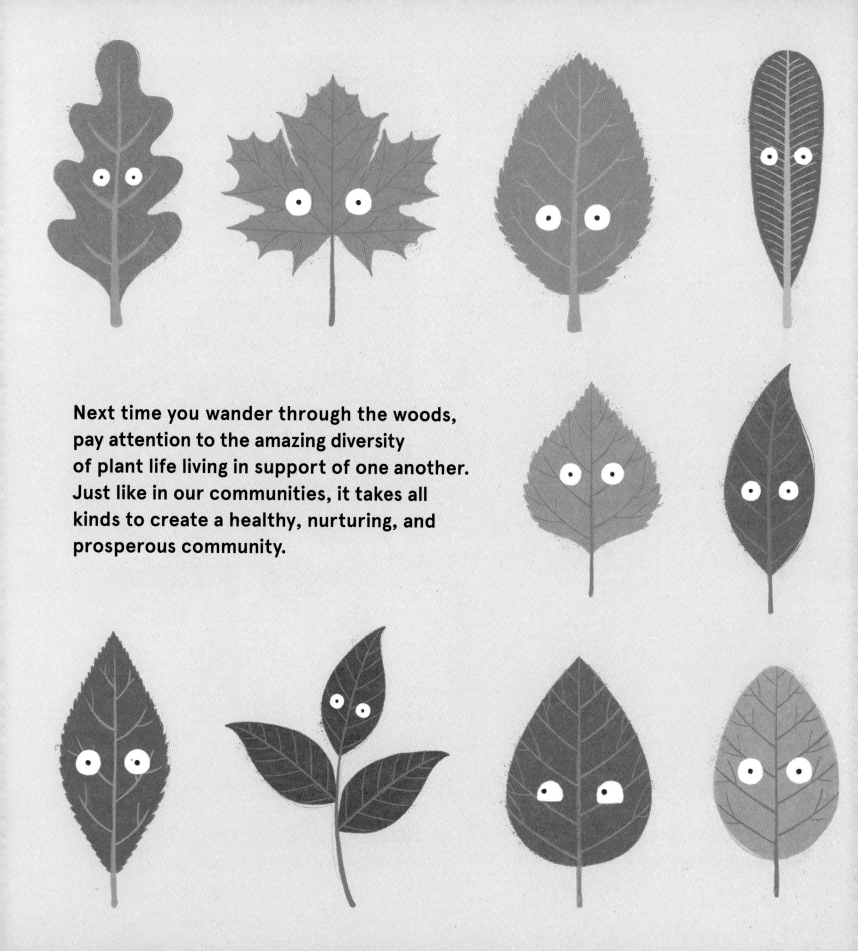

Next time you wander through the woods,
pay attention to the amazing diversity
of plant life living in support of one another.
Just like in our communities, it takes all
kinds to create a healthy, nurturing, and
prosperous community.

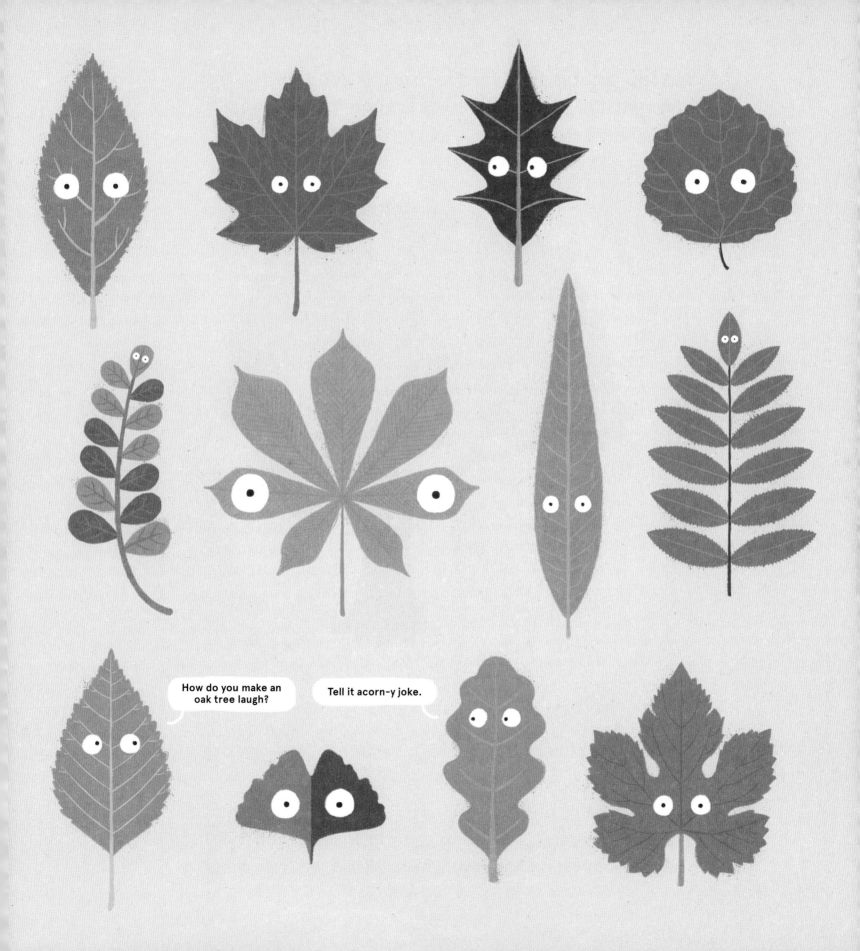

When things get a bit rough,
find the strength and flexibility
to stay centered, and hold on.

Branch out! Test many
directions, but push yourself
toward the things that
give you the most energy.

Time to make like a tree . . .

FOR EUMUNDI
STATE SCHOOL

There are around 3.4 trillion trees on our planet.
That's around 400 trees for every human. It sounds like a lot, but
at our current rate of deforestation, we're losing almost 1.5 trees
per person, per year. The best thing we can all do to help the trees
(and ourselves) is to slow down our consumption. Limit the things you buy,
plant a native tree if you can, and spend more time in the woods.

Acknowledgment of Country: I would like to acknowledge the traditional custodians of the land on which I live and work, and I pay respect
to the Gubbi Gubbi nation. I pay respects to the Elders of the community and extend my recognition to their descendants. Philip Bunting